Title: Basic learning of Computer Science and IT

A Beginner's Guide to Fundamental Concepts in Computer Science and Information Technology

Introduction

Computer science is an ever-evolving field that plays a crucial role in our daily lives. From smartphones to artificial intelligence, computing technologies impact nearly every aspect of society. This book is designed to provide a fundamental understanding of computer science, making it accessible to beginners and enthusiasts alike.

The journey begins with an overview of computers, their history, and the essential components that make them function. We then delve into the basics of hardware, software, and networking, providing foundational knowledge on how computers operate and communicate. As we progress, the book explores programming concepts, cybersecurity principles, and database management, equipping readers with essential skills for the digital age.

Emerging technologies such as artificial intelligence, cloud computing, and blockchain are also introduced, giving insight into the future of computing. Additionally, the book highlights various career paths in computer science and the skills necessary to excel in the field.

By the end of this book, readers will have a solid grasp of computer science fundamentals and be prepared to continue their exploration into more advanced topics. Whether you're an aspiring programmer, a tech enthusiast, or just curious about computers, this book serves as a stepping stone into the world of computing.

BY

Ghulam Abbas Siyal

Table of contents

Chapter 1: Understanding Computers

- ## *Definition of a Computer*

A computer is a programmable electronic device designed to accept data, perform prescribed mathematical and logical operations at high speed, and display the results of these operations.

→ It has the ability to store, retrieve, and process data, enabling users to type documents, send emails, play games, browse the web, and more.

→ Modern computers consist of at least one processing element, typically a central processing unit (CPU), and some form of memory. They also include peripheral devices for input (e.g., keyboards, mice), output (e.g., monitors, printers), and storage (e.g., hard drives, SSDs).

- ## *History of Computers*

The evolution of computers spans several centuries, marked by significant milestones that have transformed them from simple calculating devices to the powerful machines integral to modern society.

→ In the early 19th century, Charles Babbage conceptualized the Analytical Engine, a mechanical general-purpose computer. Although never completed during his lifetime, this design laid the groundwork for future computational machines.

➢ **Electromechanical Computers:**

The 1930s and 1940s saw the emergence of electromechanical computers. Konrad Zuse, a German engineer, developed the Z1 in the late 1930s, considered one of the first programmable computers. Built in his parents' living room, the Z1 utilized mechanical components and represented a significant step toward modern computing.

➢ **Electronic Computers:**

The advent of electronic components revolutionized computing. In 1944, the Colossus was developed in the United Kingdom to decrypt German messages during World War II. It is recognized as the first programmable digital computer.

→ In the United States, the ENIAC (Electronic Numerical Integrator and Computer) was completed in 1945. Weighing 30 tons and containing over 18,000 vacuum tubes, ENIAC was capable of performing complex calculations much faster than its predecessors.

➤ **Modern Computers:**

The latter half of the 20th century introduced transistors and integrated circuits, leading to smaller, more powerful, and more reliable computers. This period saw the development of personal computers, bringing computing into homes and offices worldwide. The continuous advancement in technology has led to the sophisticated and compact devices we use today, such as smartphones and tablets.

The history of computers is a testament to human ingenuity and the relentless pursuit of

• *Types of Computers*
➤ **Supercomputer:**

Supercomputers are the pinnacle of high-performance computing, designed to perform complex calculations at unprecedented speeds. They consist of thousands of interconnected nodes, each equipped with multiple processors and memory, enabling them to tackle tasks that are computationally intensive and require massive parallel processing.

Key Characteristics of Supercomputers:

→ **Parallel Processing:** Supercomputers divide large computational problems into smaller   tasks and process them simultaneously across numerous processors, significantly reducing the time required to reach a solution.
→ **High-Speed Interconnects:** The nodes within a supercomputer are connected through high-speed networks, ensuring rapid data transfer and efficient communication between processors.
→ **Massive Storage Systems:** To handle the vast amounts of data processed, supercomputers are equipped with extensive storage solutions that provide quick data retrieval and storage capabilities.

Applications of Supercomputers:

Supercomputers are utilized in various fields that require substantial computational power, including:

→ **Scientific Research:** Modeling and simulating complex systems such as climate patterns, astrophysical phenomena, and molecular structures.
→ **Engineering:** Designing and testing new materials, aerodynamics simulations, and structural analysis.
→ **Healthcare:** Genomic sequencing, drug discovery, and personalized medicine development.
→ **Artificial Intelligence:** Training large-scale AI models and conducting deep learning research.

➢ Mainframes computer:

Mainframe computers, often referred to as "big iron," are powerful machines primarily utilized by large organizations for critical applications such as bulk data processing, enterprise resource planning, and large-scale transaction processing.

Key Characteristics of Mainframe Computers:

→ **High Performance:** Designed to handle vast amounts of data and support thousands of users simultaneously, mainframes excel in processing large-scale computations and transactions efficiently.

→ **Reliability and Availability:** Mainframes are engineered for maximum uptime, often achieving availability levels exceeding 99.99%, making them ideal for mission-critical operations.

→ **Scalability:** They can be scaled to accommodate increasing workloads without compromising performance, ensuring they meet evolving business demands.

→ **Security:** Mainframes offer robust security features, including advanced encryption and access controls, safeguarding sensitive data against unauthorized access.

Applications of Mainframe Computers:

→ **Financial Services:** Banks and insurance companies rely on mainframes for processing transactions, managing accounts, and handling large-scale financial data.

→ **Government Agencies:** Used for census data processing, tax records management, and other large-scale public data operations.

→ **Retail:** Mainframes manage inventory, sales transactions, and supply chain logistics for large retail chains.

→ **Healthcare:** Hospitals and healthcare providers utilize mainframes to store and manage vast amounts of patient data securely.

➢ Personal computers:

Personal computers (PCs) are digital devices designed for individual use, enabling users to perform a variety of tasks such as word processing, internet browsing, gaming, and multimedia consumption. They have become an integral part of daily life, serving both personal and professional needs.

Key Characteristics of Personal Computers:

→ **User-Friendly Interface:** Designed for ease of use, PCs feature graphical user interfaces (GUIs) that allow users to interact with the system through visual elements like icons and menus.

→ **Versatility:** Personal computers support a wide range of applications, from productivity software and educational programs to entertainment and creative tools.

→ **Affordability:** Over the years, advancements in technology have made PCs more affordable, making them accessible to a broad audience.

Types of Personal Computers:

→ **Desktop Computers:** These consist of separate components, including a tower (which houses the CPU, memory, and storage), monitor, keyboard, and mouse. Desktops are known for their performance capabilities and are often used in settings where mobility is not a primary concern.

→ **Laptops:** Portable computers that integrate the display, keyboard, and processing components into a single unit. Laptops offer the advantage of mobility

• *Basic Components of a Computer (CPU, RAM, Storage, Input/Output Devices)*

➢ **CPU:**

The Central Processing Unit (CPU) is the primary component of a computer that interprets and executes instructions, effectively serving as the "brain" of the system. It performs essential operations such as arithmetic calculations, logical decision-making, and data management, enabling the computer to run programs and process information.

A CPU typically consists of several key components:

→ **Control Unit (CU):** Directs the operation of the processor by interpreting instructions and initiating appropriate actions.

→ **Arithmetic Logic Unit (ALU):** Handles mathematical computations and logical operations.

→ **Registers:** Small, high-speed storage locations within the CPU that temporarily hold data, instructions, and addresses during processing.

→ **Cache:** A specialized form of memory that stores frequently accessed data to speed up processing tasks.

Modern CPUs often feature multiple cores, allowing them to process multiple instructions simultaneously, thereby enhancing performance. They also support various instruction sets and modes to efficiently manage tasks and interact with other computers.

➢ **RAM:**

Random Access Memory (RAM) is a crucial component in computing systems, serving as the short-term memory where data and instructions are stored temporarily for quick access by the Central Processing Unit (CPU). Unlike long-term storage devices such as hard drives or solid-state drives, RAM is volatile; it retains data only while the computer is powered on. Once the system is turned off, all data stored in RAM is lost.

→ The primary function of RAM is to provide fast read and write access to data that the CPU needs immediately. This rapid access speeds up the execution of programs and enhances overall system performance. For instance, when running applications or opening files, the necessary data is loaded into RAM from the storage device, allowing the CPU to process it efficiently.

➜ There are different types of RAM, including Dynamic RAM (DRAM) and Static RAM (SRAM). DRAM is commonly used in personal computers due to its cost-effectiveness and higher storage capacity, while SRAM is faster and more reliable but typically used in smaller quantities for specific applications like CPU caches.

➤ Computer storage:

Computer storage refers to the various methods and technologies used to capture and retain digital information on electromagnetic, optical, or silicon-based media. It enables computers to store data and programs, facilitating their retrieval and manipulation.

There are two primary types of computer storage:

➜ **Primary Storage (Volatile):** This includes Random Access Memory (RAM), which temporarily holds data and instructions that the CPU needs while performing tasks. RAM is fast but loses its contents when the computer is powered off.

➜ **Secondary Storage (Non-Volatile):** This encompasses devices that retain data even when the computer is turned off. Common examples include Hard Disk Drives (HDDs), Solid State Drives (SSDs), optical discs like CDs and DVDs, and flash drives. These devices offer larger storage capacities compared to primary storage and are used for long-term data storage.

➜ The choice of storage device depends on factors such as speed, capacity, cost, and intended use. For instance, SSDs provide faster data access speeds than HDDs but are typically more expensive. Optical discs are less commonly used today due to their lower storage capacity and slower data transfer rates.

• _Input and Output (I/O) devices_

Input and Output (I/O) devices are essential hardware components that enable interaction between a computer system and the external environment, facilitating data exchange between the user and the machine.

➤ Input Devices:

These devices allow users to enter data into a computer. Common examples include:

➜ **Keyboard:** Enables users to input text and commands.
➜ **Mouse:** Allows users to interact with graphical elements on the screen.
➜ **Scanner:** Converts physical documents into digital formats.
➜ **Microphone:** Captures audio input for recording or communication purposes.
➜ **Webcam:** Captures video input for streaming or recording.

➢ Output Devices:

These devices enable the computer to present data to the user. Common examples include:

- ➢ **Monitor:** Displays visual output, including text, images, and videos.
- ➢ **Printer:** Produces physical copies of digital documents.
- ➢ **Speakers:** Emit audio output, such as music or system sounds.
- ➢ **Headphones:** Provide personal audio output for the user.

➢ Input/Output Devices:

Some devices perform both input and output functions, facilitating bidirectional data exchange. Examples include:

- → **Touchscreen:** Allows users to input data through touch and provides visual output.
- → **Network Interface Card (NIC):** Enables data transmission to and from the computer over a network.
- → **External Storage Devices (e.g., USB flash drives):** Allow data to be written to and read from the device.

Chapter 2: Fundamentals of Computer Hardware

- ## *Central Processing Unit (CPU) and Its Functions*

The Central Processing Unit (CPU) is the primary component of a computer responsible for interpreting and executing instructions. Its core functions include:

→ **Fetching Instructions:** The CPU retrieves instructions from the computer's memory to process tasks.

→ **Decoding Instructions:** Once fetched, the CPU deciphers these instructions to determine the required actions.

→ **Executing Instructions:** The CPU performs the necessary operations, which may involve arithmetic calculations, logical comparisons, or data movement

→ **Storing Results:** After execution, the CPU stores the results back into memory or registers for future use.

These functions are orchestrated by the CPU's internal components:

→ **Control Unit (CU):** Directs operations within the processor, managing the flow of data and instructions.

→ **Arithmetic Logic Unit (ALU):** Handles mathematical computations and logical operations.

- ## *Memory and Storage Devices*
➢ **Memory:**

Often referred to as **Random Access Memory (RAM)**, memory provides temporary storage that the CPU utilizes to store data that is actively being used or processed. This allows for quick access and manipulation, enhancing system performance. However, RAM is volatile, meaning it loses all stored information when the computer is powered off.

➢ **Storage Devices:**

Storage devices are responsible for the long-term retention of data, preserving information even when the computer is turned off. They come in various forms, including:

→ **Hard Disk Drives (HDDs):** Utilize spinning magnetic disks to read and write data.

→ **Solid State Drives (SSDs):** Employ flash memory to store data, offering faster access speeds and greater durability compared to HDDs.

→ **Optical Discs:** Such as CDs, DVDs, and Blu-ray discs, which use laser technology to read and write data.

→ **USB Flash Drives:** Portable storage devices that use flash memory for data storage.

→ **Cloud Storage:** Allows data to be stored on remote servers accessed via the internet, providing scalability and remote accessibility.

Understanding the differences between memory and storage is crucial for optimizing computer performance and ensuring efficient data management. Memory (RAM) offers rapid access for active processes but is temporary, while storage devices provide permanent data retention, essential for preserving files and applications over time.

- ## _Motherboard and Power Supply_

The **motherboard** and **power supply unit (PSU)** are essential components in a computer system, each playing a critical role in its operation.

➢ Motherboard:

The motherboard serves as the main circuit board, connecting and facilitating communication between all hardware components, including the CPU, RAM, storage devices, and peripheral interfaces. It also manages power distribution to these components, ensuring stable and efficient operation. A key feature of the motherboard is the Voltage Regulator Module (VRM), which regulates voltage levels to meet the specific requirements of the CPU and other components.

➢ Power Supply Unit (PSU):

The PSU is responsible for converting the alternating current (AC) from an electrical outlet into direct current (DC) that the computer components require. It supplies and regulates the necessary voltages to the motherboard, adapters, and peripheral devices, ensuring they receive consistent and safe power. Additionally, the PSU contributes to system cooling by facilitating airflow through the computer case.

→ In summary, the motherboard acts as the central hub that connects and manages communication between all computer components, while the PSU provides and regulates the power needed for their operation.

Chapter 3: Basics of Software

- ## *Definition of Software*

Software refers to a set of instructions, data, or programs used to operate computers and execute specific tasks. It is the intangible counterpart to hardware, which encompasses the physical components of a computer system.

Types of Software (System Software, Application Software, Utility Software)

- ➢ **System Software:** This includes operating systems and utilities that manage and support a computer's basic functions, such as managing hardware resources and providing a platform for application software.
- ➢ **Application Software:** These are programs designed to help users perform specific tasks, such as word processing, web browsing, or playing games.
- ➢ **Utility Software:** Utility software is a type of system software designed to help manage, maintain, and optimize computer systems. Unlike application software, which performs tasks directly benefiting users, utility programs focus on supporting the computer infrastructure.

- ## *Operating Systems (Windows, macOS, Linux)*

Operating systems (OS) are essential software that manage computer hardware and software resources, providing services for computer programs. The three most prevalent desktop operating systems are **Microsoft Windows**, **macOS**, and **Linux**.

- ➢ **Microsoft Windows:**

Developed by Microsoft, Windows is a proprietary operating system widely used on personal computers, laptops, tablets, and workstations. It is known for its user-friendly interface and broad software compatibility. Windows supports a vast array of applications, making it versatile for both personal and professional use. As of 2024, Windows holds a significant share of the desktop OS market.

- ➢ **macOS:**

Created by Apple Inc., macOS is the operating system exclusively for Mac computers. It is recognized for its sleek design, strong performance, and seamless integration with other Apple products and services. macOS offers a consistent and intuitive user experience, appealing to users who value aesthetics and simplicity. In 2024, macOS maintained a notable presence in the desktop OS market.

- ➢ **Linux:**

Linux is an open-source operating system distributed under the GNU General Public License (GPL), allowing users to freely use, modify, and distribute its source code. Designed by programmers for their own use, Linux emphasizes simplicity and consistency. It is favored by developers and system administrators for its flexibility, security, and robustness. Linux is widely used in server environments and powers the majority of the world's supercomputers.

→ Each of these operating systems offers unique features and caters to different user preferences and requirements. The choice among them depends on factors such as hardware compatibility, software needs, and personal or organizational priorities.

- ### *Introduction to Programming Languages*

Programming languages are formal systems of notation that enable humans to communicate instructions to computers. They consist of a set of symbols, syntax rules, and semantics that define how to write programs to perform specific tasks. By using programming languages, developers can create software applications, control hardware devices, and process data efficiently.

Programming languages can be broadly categorized based on their level of abstraction:

1. **Low-Level Languages:** These languages are closer to machine code and provide little abstraction from a computer's instruction set architecture. They include:
   - **Machine Language:** The most basic language, consisting of binary code that the computer's central processing unit (CPU) can execute directly.
   - **Assembly Language:** A slight abstraction over machine language, using mnemonic codes to represent machine-level instructions, making it more readable for humans.
2. **High-Level Languages:** These languages offer greater abstraction, making them more user-friendly and easier to write, read, and maintain. They are platform-independent and include languages such as:
   - **Procedural Languages:** Focus on a sequence of procedural steps to execute, e.g., C.
   - **Object-Oriented Languages:** Center around objects and classes, promoting modularity and reusability, e.g., Java, C++.
   - **Functional Languages:** Emphasize the evaluation of expressions rather than the execution of commands, e.g., Haskell, Lisp.
   - **Scripting Languages:** Often used for writing scripts that automate tasks, e.g., JavaScript, PHP.

Each programming language is designed with specific goals and is suited to particular types of tasks. The choice of language depends on factors such as the problem domain, performance requirements, and the development environment.

Chapter 4: Introduction to Computer Networks

- ## *What is a Network?*

A **computer network** is a system that connects multiple computing devices to facilitate the exchange of data and resources. These connections can be established using wired media, such as cables, or wireless technologies.

→ Networks enable devices to communicate and share resources efficiently. For instance, in a client-server network, client devices like personal computers or smartphones request data or services from centralized servers, which store and manage resources such as files, applications, or websites.

- ## *Types of Networks (LAN, WAN, MAN)*

Computer networks are categorized based on their geographic scope and purpose. The primary types include Local Area Networks (LAN), Metropolitan Area Networks (MAN), and Wide Area Networks (WAN).

➢ ### Local Area Network (LAN):

A LAN connects devices within a limited area, such as a home, office, or campus. It facilitates high-speed data transfer and resource sharing among connected devices. LANs are typically owned and managed by a single organization.

➢ ### Metropolitan Area Network (MAN):

A MAN spans a larger area than a LAN, covering a city or a large campus. It connects multiple LANs to create a network that enables resource sharing and communication across various locations within the metropolitan area. MANs are often used by organizations with multiple offices in the same city.

➢ ### Wide Area Network (WAN):

A WAN covers a broad geographic area, such as a country or continent. It connects multiple LANs and MANs, facilitating communication and resource sharing over long distances. The internet is the most well-known example of a WAN.

- ## *Internet and How It Works*

The **Internet** is a vast global network that connects millions of private, public, academic, business, and government networks, enabling devices worldwide to communicate and share information.

How the Internet Works:

1. **Data Transmission:** Information on the Internet is transmitted using the Transmission Control Protocol/Internet Protocol (TCP/IP) suite. Data is broken into smaller units called "packets," each containing a portion of the overall information along with metadata like source and destination addresses.
2. **Routing:** These packets travel through a series of routers, which direct them toward their destination by determining the most efficient path across interconnected networks. Each router examines the packet's destination address and forwards it accordingly, often passing through multiple routers before reaching the target devices.
3. **Reassembly:** Once all packets arrive at the destination, the receiving device reassembles them into the original data using TCP, ensuring that the information is complete and correctly ordered.

This process allows for reliable and efficient communication across the globe, enabling various services such as web browsing, email, and file sharing.

- ## *Network Protocols (TCP/IP, HTTP, FTP)*

Network protocols are standardized rules that govern how data is transmitted and received across networks, ensuring devices can communicate effectively. Three fundamental protocols in this domain are **TCP/IP**, **HTTP**, and **FTP**.

➤ **TCP/IP (Transmission Control Protocol/Internet Protocol):**

TCP/IP is the foundational suite of protocols for internet communication. It enables devices to connect and communicate over the internet by defining how data packets are transmitted and routed. TCP ensures reliable, ordered, and error-checked delivery of data between systems, while IP handles the routing of data packets across networks, directing them from sender to receiver using IP addresses.

➤ **HTTP (Hypertext Transfer Protocol):**

HTTP is the protocol used for transferring web pages on the internet. When you access a website, your browser uses HTTP to request and receive web pages from servers. It operates over TCP/IP and is essential for web browsing, enabling the retrieval of HTML documents, images, and other resources

> **FTP (File Transfer Protocol):**

FTP is used for transferring files between computers on a network. It allows users to upload and download files to and from servers, facilitating the sharing and management of files across networks. FTP operates over TCP/IP and is commonly used for website maintenance, data backup, and sharing large files.

→ Understanding these protocols is crucial for comprehending how data is transmitted and managed across networks, forming the backbone of internet communication and file sharing.

Chapter 5: Basics of Cybersecurity

- ## *<u>Importance of Cybersecurity</u>*

    Cybersecurity is the practice of protecting systems, networks, and data from digital attacks, unauthorized access, damage, or theft. In today's digital age, where individuals and organizations rely heavily on technology, the importance of cybersecurity cannot be overstated.

    ➤ Key Reasons Why Cybersecurity is Crucial:
    → **Protection of Sensitive Data:**
    → **Prevention of Financial Losses:**
    → **Maintaining Reputation and Trust**
    → **Ensuring Operational Continuity:**
    → **Compliance with Regulations:**

- ## *<u>Common Cyber Threats (Malware, Phishing, Ransomware)</u>*

    Cyber threats are malicious activities aimed at compromising the confidentiality, integrity, and availability of information systems. Among the most prevalent are **Malware**, **Phishing**, and **Ransomware**.

    ➤ **Malware:**

    Malware, short for malicious software, encompasses various harmful programs designed to damage, disrupt, or gain unauthorized access to computer systems. Common types include viruses, worms, trojans, spyware, and adware. These programs can steal sensitive information, corrupt data, or provide unauthorized access to attackers.

    ➤ **Phishing:**

    Phishing involves deceptive communications, often via email, that appear to come from reputable sources. The goal is to trick individuals into revealing confidential information such as login credentials, credit card numbers, or other personal data. Phishing attacks frequently use urgent or alarming messages to prompt quick action from the recipient.

    ➤ **Ransomware:**

    Ransomware is a type of malware that encrypts a victim's files or locks them out of their system, with the attacker demanding payment (ransom) for decryption or restoration of access. These attacks can cause significant operational disruptions and financial losses.

    → Understanding these threats is crucial for implementing effective cybersecurity measures to protect personal and organizational data.

● *Introduction to Encryption*

Encryption is the process of converting readable data, known as plaintext, into an unreadable format called ciphertext. This transformation ensures that only authorized parties, possessing the correct decryption key, can access the original information. Encryption is fundamental to securing sensitive data, maintaining privacy, and protecting information integrity across various applications, including online communications, financial transactions, and data storage.

There are two primary types of encryption:

1. **Symmetric Encryption:** This method uses a single key for both encryption and decryption. While it is efficient and fast, the key must be securely shared between the communicating parties to prevent unauthorized access.
2. **Asymmetric Encryption:** Also known as public-key cryptography, this approach employs a pair of keys: a public key, which is shared openly, and a private key, which remains confidential. Data encrypted with the public key can only be decrypted by the corresponding private key, enhancing security by eliminating the need to share secret keys.

Chapter 6: Introduction to Programming

- ## *What is Programming?*

Programming is the process of creating a set of instructions, known as code, that a computer can execute to perform specific tasks or solve problems. This involves writing, testing, debugging, and maintaining code in various programming languages, such as Python, Java, or C++. Programming enables the development of software applications, websites, and systems that drive modern technology.

→ At its core, programming is about translating human ideas and logic into a language that computers can understand and act upon. This process encompasses several key activities:

→ **Designing Algorithms:** Developing step-by-step procedures or formulas to solve specific problems.

→ **Writing Code:** Implementing algorithms using programming languages.

→ **Testing and Debugging:** Identifying and fixing errors or bugs in the code to ensure it functions as intended.

→ **Maintaining and Updating:** Modifying code to improve performance, add features, or adapt to new requirements.

- ## I*ntroduction to Algorithms and Flowcharts*

Algorithms and **flowcharts** are fundamental tools in computer science and programming, serving as blueprints for problem-solving and system design.

➢ **Algorithms:**

An algorithm is a step-by-step procedure or formula for solving a problem. It provides a clear, logical sequence of actions to achieve a specific goal, ensuring consistency and efficiency in problem-solving. Algorithms can be expressed in natural language, pseudocode, or formal programming languages, and they form the basis for developing software applications and systems.

➢ **Flowcharts:**

A flowchart is a diagrammatic representation of an algorithm, using various symbols and arrows to depict the flow of control and data within a process. This visual tool helps in understanding, analyzing, and communicating the logic of a system or process, making it easier to identify potential issues and optimize performance.

- ## *Basics of a Programming Language (Variables, Data Types, Loops, Conditions)*

Understanding the fundamentals of programming is essential for anyone looking to delve into software development. The core concepts include **variables**, **data types**, **loops**, and **conditions**.

➢ **Variables:**

Variables are named storage locations in a program that hold data values. They act as containers for data that can change during the execution of a program. For example, in the statement *int x = 10;*, x is a variable of type *int* (integer), and it is assigned the value 10.

➢ **Data Types:**

Data types define the kind of data a variable can hold. Common data types include:

→ **Integer (*int*):** Represents whole numbers.

→ **Floating-point (*float*):** Represents numbers with decimal points.

→ **Character (*char*):** Represents single characters.

→ **String (*string*):** Represents sequences of characters.

→ **Boolean (*bool*):** Represents *true* or *false* values.

Choosing the appropriate data type is crucial for efficient memory usage and accurate data representation.

➢ **Loops:**

Loops are control structures that allow a set of instructions to be executed repeatedly based on a condition. They are essential for performing repetitive tasks without redundant code. Common types of loops include:

→ **For Loop:** Repeats a block of code a specific number of times.
→ **While Loop:** Repeats a block of code as long as a specified condition is true.
→ **Do-While Loop:** Similar to the while loop, but guarantees at least one execution of the code block.

For example, a *for* loop in C++ that prints numbers from 1 to 5:

cpp

CopyEdit

```
for (int i = 1; i <= 5; i++) {

    cout << i << endl;

}
```

Loops are fundamental for tasks that require repetition, such as processing items in a list or performing calculations multiple times.

➤ **Conditions:**

Conditions, or conditional statements, allow a program to execute certain blocks of code based on whether a specified condition is true or false. The most common conditional statement is the *if* statement, which can be combined with *else* and *else if* to handle multiple scenarios.

For example, an *if* statement in Python that checks if a number is positive:

python

CopyEdit

```
if number > 0:

    print("Positive number")

else:

    print("Non-positive number")
```

→ Conditional statements are essential for decision-making processes in programs, enabling them to respond differently under various conditions.
→ Mastering these basic constructs is the foundation for writing effective and efficient code in any programming language.

- ***Introduction of Python***

Writing simple code in Python is an excellent way to begin your programming journey due to its readability and straightforward syntax.

Here's a step-by-step guide to creating a basic Python program:

➤ **Setting Up Your Environment:**

Before writing Python code, ensure that Python is installed on your system. After installation, you can write Python code using any text editor or an Integrated Development Environment (IDE) like PyCharm or VS Code.

➢ Writing Your First Python Program:

A traditional first program in many languages is one that prints "Hello, World!" to the screen. Here's how you can do it in Python:

python

CopyEdit

```
print("Hello, World!")
```

Save this code in a file with a *.py* extension, such as *hello_world.py*. To run the program, open your command line or terminal, navigate to the directory containing your file, and execute:

bash

CopyEdit

```
python hello_world.py
```

This will display:

CopyEdit

```
Hello, World!
```

➢ Understanding the Code:
→ *print()*: This is a built-in Python function that outputs the specified message to the screen.

→ *"Hello, World!"*: This is a string, a sequence of characters enclosed in quotes.

➢ Expanding Your Program:

To make your program more interactive, you can prompt the user for input and display a personalized message:

python

CopyEdit

```
name = input("Enter your name: ")

print(f"Hello, {name}!")
```

In this program:

→ *input()*: This function prompts the user for input and returns it as a string.

→ *name*: A variable that stores the user's input.

→ *print(f"Hello, {name}!")*: This uses an f-string to embed the value of *name* into the string, creating a personalized greeting.

> **Running the Expanded Program:**

Save this code in a file, such as *greet_user.py*, and run it in the same manner as before. The program will prompt you to enter your name and then greet you accordingly.

By practicing these simple programs, you'll build a solid foundation in Python programming, enabling you to tackle more complex projects in the future.

Chapter 7: Databases and Data Management

- ## *What is a Database?*

A **database** is an organized collection of data stored electronically in a computer system. It allows for efficient storage, retrieval, and management of information, which can include text, numbers, images, and other types of files. Databases are essential for applications ranging from simple data storage to complex data analysis.

Key Components of a Database:

→ **Data:** The actual information stored, such as customer records, product details, or transaction histories.

→ **Database Management System (DBMS):** Software that interacts with end-users, applications, and the database itself to capture and analyze data. It provides tools for creating, reading, updating, and deleting data.

→ **Schemas:** The structure that defines the organization of data, including tables, fields, and relationships between tables.

- ## *Types of Databases (Relational, NoSQL)*

There are several types of database:

> ### Relational Databases:

Store data in tables with rows and columns, using Structured Query Language (SQL) for data management.

> ### Non-Relational Databases:

Also known as NoSQL databases, they store data in various formats like key-value pairs, documents, or graphs, and are designed for scalability and flexibility.

- ## *Introduction to SQL*

Structured Query Language (SQL) is a standardized programming language designed for managing and manipulating relational databases. It enables users to perform various operations such as querying data, updating records, and managing database structures.

Key Features of SQL:

→ **Data Querying:** Retrieve specific information from databases using the *SELECT* statement.

→ **Data Manipulation:** Insert new records (*INSERT*), update existing records (*UPDATE*), and delete records (*DELETE*).

→ **Database Management:** Create and modify database structures, including tables and indexes (*CREATE, ALTER, DROP*).

→ **Access Control:** Define user permissions and security levels (*GRANT, REVOKE*).

Common SQL Commands:

→ *SELECT*: Retrieves data from one or more tables.

→ *INSERT INTO*: Adds new records to a table.

→ *UPDATE*: Modifies existing records.

→ *DELETE*: Removes records from a table.

→ *CREATE TABLE*: Defines a new table along with its columns and data types.

→ *ALTER TABLE*: Modifies an existing table's structure.

→ *DROP TABLE*: Deletes a table from the database.

Example: Retrieving Data

To retrieve all records from a table named *Employees*:

sql

CopyEdit

*SELECT * FROM Employees;*

This command fetches all columns and rows from the *Employees* table.

- ## *Basics of Data Storage and Retrieval*

Data storage and retrieval are fundamental concepts in computing, enabling systems to save, access, and manage information efficiently.

➢ **Data Storage:**

Data storage involves saving digital information on various media to ensure its preservation and future access. This process utilizes magnetic, optical, or mechanical media to record and maintain data for ongoing or future operations.

→ **Types of Data Storage:**
1. **Primary Storage (Volatile):**
   ○ **Random Access Memory (RAM):** Temporary storage that holds data and instructions currently in use. Its contents are lost when the system is powered off.

2. **Secondary Storage (Non-Volatile):**
   ○ **Hard Disk Drives (HDDs):** Mechanical devices that store data on spinning disks. They offer large storage capacities but are slower compared to newer technologies.
   ○ **Solid-State Drives (SSDs):** Use flash memory to store data, providing faster access speeds and greater durability than HDDs.
   ○ **Optical Discs:** Media like CDs and DVDs that use laser technology to read and write data.
3. **Tertiary and Off-line Storage:**
   ○ **Tertiary Storage:** Involves robotic systems that automatically load and unload storage media, such as tape libraries, suitable for archiving large amounts of data.
   ○ **Off-line Storage:** Data is stored on removable media like external hard drives or tapes, requiring manual intervention to access.

➢ **Data Retrieval:**

Data retrieval is the process of accessing stored information. Efficient retrieval depends on the storage medium's speed and the system's ability to locate and process the data. For example, accessing data from an SSD is faster than from an HDD due to the absence of moving parts.

Chapter 8: Emerging Technologies

➤ *Artificial Intelligence and Machine Learning*

Artificial Intelligence (AI) refers to the simulation of human intelligence in machines designed to think, learn, and perform tasks autonomously. AI encompasses various subfields, including machine learning, natural language processing, robotics, and computer vision. Its applications are vast, ranging from virtual assistants and recommendation systems to autonomous vehicles and advanced data analytics.

→ **Machine Learning (ML)** is a subset of AI that enables systems to learn from data and improve their performance over time without explicit programming. ML algorithms identify patterns within data, allowing machines to make predictions or decisions based on new, unseen information. Common types of machine learning include supervised learning, unsupervised learning, and reinforcement learning.

Key Differences Between AI and ML:

→ **Scope:** AI is the overarching field focused on creating intelligent systems, while ML is a specific approach within AI that uses data-driven methods to achieve intelligence.
→ **Functionality:** AI systems aim to mimic human cognitive functions, whereas ML systems learn from data to perform tasks without being explicitly programmed.

Understanding the distinction between AI and ML is crucial for comprehending how intelligent systems are developed and the methodologies they employ to solve complex problems.

➤ *Cloud Computing:*

Cloud computing is the delivery of computing services—including servers, storage, databases, networking, software, analytics, and intelligence—over the internet ("the cloud") to offer faster innovation, flexible resources, and economies of scale. You typically pay only for cloud services you use, helping you lower your operating costs, run your infrastructure more efficiently, and scale as your business needs change.

Key Characteristics of Cloud Computing:

➤ **On-Demand Self-Service:** Users can provision computing resources automatically without requiring human intervention with each service provider.
➤ **Broad Network Access:** Capabilities are available over the network and accessed through standard mechanisms that promote use by heterogeneous client platforms.
➤ **Resource Pooling:** The provider's computing resources are pooled to serve multiple consumers using a multi-tenant model, with different physical and virtual resources dynamically assigned and reassigned according to consumer demand.
➤ **Rapid Elasticity:** Capabilities can be elastically provisioned and released, in some cases automatically, to scale rapidly outward and inward commensurate with demand.
➤ **Measured Service:** Cloud systems automatically control and optimize resource use by leveraging metering capability at some level of abstraction appropriate to the type of service.

- ***what is Blockchain Technology:***

Blockchain Technology**Blockchain technology** is a decentralized digital ledger system that securely records transactions across a network of computers. Each "block" contains a set of transactions, and these blocks are linked together in a chronological "chain," ensuring data integrity and transparency. Once a block is added, it cannot be altered retroactively without consensus from the network, making blockchain highly resistant to tampering and fraud.

Key Features of Blockchain:

→ **Decentralization:** Unlike traditional centralized databases, blockchain operates on a peer-to-peer network, distributing control and reducing the risk of a single point of failure.
→ **Transparency:** Transactions are visible to all participants in the network, promoting trust and accountability.
→ **Immutability:** Once recorded, data cannot be changed or deleted, ensuring a permanent and tamper-proof record.
→ **Security:** Advanced cryptographic techniques protect data, making unauthorized access or alterations extremely difficult.

Applications of Blockchain:

→ **Cryptocurrencies:** Blockchain underpins digital currencies like Bitcoin and Ethereum, enabling secure and transparent financial transactions.
→ **Supply Chain Management:** It allows for real-time tracking of products from origin to delivery, enhancing transparency and efficiency.
→ **Smart Contracts:** Blockchain facilitates self-executing contracts with terms directly written into code, automating processes and reducing the need for intermediaries.
→ **Healthcare:** It can securely store and share patient records, improving data accessibility and privacy.

➢ ***The Future of Computing***

The future of computing is poised for transformative advancements, driven by several key technologies:

1. Artificial Intelligence (AI) and Machine Learning (ML):

AI and ML are set to revolutionize computing by enabling systems to learn from data and make autonomous decisions. Prominent AI scientist Yann LeCun predicts significant advancements in AI technology within the next 3-5 years, essential for developing domestic robots and fully autonomous vehicles.

2. Quantum Computing:

Quantum computing leverages the principles of quantum mechanics to process information in fundamentally new ways. This technology holds the potential to solve complex problems beyond the capabilities of classical computers, impacting fields such as cryptography, optimization, and drug discovery.

3. Blockchain Technology:

Blockchain offers a decentralized and secure method for recording transactions and managing data. Its applications extend beyond cryptocurrencies, influencing sectors like supply chain management, healthcare, and finance by enhancing transparency and security.

4. Advanced Computing Architectures:

The development of specialized hardware, such as neuromorphic and quantum processors, is expected to drive the next generation of computing. These architectures aim to mimic human brain functions and harness quantum mechanics to process information more efficiently.

5. Integration of Computing and Neuroscience:

Future computing systems may integrate principles from neuroscience, leading to more efficient and adaptable computing models. This convergence could result in systems that better emulate human cognitive processes, enhancing machine learning and AI capabilities.

Chapter 9: Careers in Computer Science

- ## _Different Fields in Computer Science (Software Development, Data Science, Cybersecurity, etc.)_

Computer science encompasses various specialized fields, each addressing distinct aspects of technology and its applications. Here's an overview of some key areas:

➢ **Software Development:**

This field focuses on designing, coding, testing, and maintaining software applications. Professionals in software development create programs that meet specific user needs, ranging from mobile apps to enterprise systems. Roles include software engineers, application developers, and systems analysts.

➢ **Data Science:**

Data science involves extracting meaningful insights from large datasets using statistical analysis, machine learning, and data visualization techniques. It's crucial for informed decision-making across various industries. Careers in this field include data scientists, data analysts, and machine learning engineers.

➢ **Cybersecurity:**

Cybersecurity focuses on protecting systems, networks, and data from digital attacks, unauthorized access, and damage. Professionals work to safeguard information and maintain the integrity of digital infrastructures. Roles encompass security analysts, ethical hackers, and cryptographers.

- ## _Skills Required for a Career in Computing_

Embarking on a career in computing requires a blend of technical expertise and soft skills. Here's an overview of essential skills:

1. Technical Skills:

→ **Programming and Coding:** Proficiency in languages such as Python, Java, C++, and JavaScript is fundamental. The ability to write clean, efficient, and maintainable code is essential.
→ **Data Analysis:** Skills in analyzing and interpreting data are crucial, especially for roles in data science and analytics. Familiarity with tools like SQL and statistical software is beneficial.
→ **Software Development:** Understanding the software development lifecycle, including design, coding, testing, and maintenance, is vital. Experience with development frameworks and version control systems is advantageous.

→ **Cybersecurity:** Knowledge of security protocols, threat analysis, and risk management is essential to protect systems and data. Familiarity with encryption methods and security tools is beneficial.

→ **Cloud Computing:** Understanding cloud platforms like AWS, Google Cloud, or Microsoft Azure is increasingly important as businesses migrate to cloud environments.

2. Soft Skills:

- **Problem-Solving and Analytical Thinking:** The ability to approach complex issues methodically and develop effective solutions is crucial.
- **Communication Skills:** Clear communication is vital for collaborating with teams, explaining technical concepts to non-technical stakeholders, and documenting processes.
- **Adaptability and Continuous Learning:** The tech industry evolves rapidly; staying updated with new technologies and methodologies is essential.
- **Teamwork and Collaboration:** Many projects require working in teams; being able to collaborate effectively is important.

- ***How to Start Learning Computer Science***

Embarking on a journey to learn computer science is both exciting and rewarding. Here's a structured approach to guide you:

1. Understand the Fundamentals:

→ **Explore Core Concepts:** Begin with foundational topics such as algorithms, data structures, computer architecture, and operating systems. These are essential for grasping how computers function and process information.

→ **Learn Programming Languages:** Start with languages like Python or JavaScript, which are beginner-friendly and widely used. Mastering programming is crucial for implementing algorithms and solving problems.

2. Utilize Online Resources:

→ **Interactive Platforms:** Engage with platforms like Codecademy, which offer interactive coding lessons and projects. This hands-on approach helps reinforce learning through practice.

→ **Structured Courses:** Consider enrolling in online courses from reputable institutions. Websites like Coursera and edX provide courses on various computer science topics, often taught by university professors.

3. Practice Regularly:

→ **Solve Problems:** Regularly tackle coding challenges on platforms like LeetCode or HackerRank to enhance your problem-solving skills. Consistent practice is key to mastering programming.
→ **Build Projects:** Apply your knowledge by creating small projects, such as a personal website or a simple game. This not only solidifies your learning but also builds a portfolio to showcase your skills.

4. Join Communities:

→ **Engage with Peers:** Participate in online forums like Stack Overflow or Reddit's r/learnprogramming to ask questions, share knowledge, and learn from others' experiences. Community engagement can provide support and motivation.
→ **Attend Workshops and Meetups:** Look for local or virtual coding workshops and meetups to network with professionals and fellow learners. These events can offer valuable insights and opportunities for collaboration.

5. Stay Curious and Updated:

→ **Explore Specializations:** As you progress, delve into areas like artificial intelligence, cybersecurity, or data science to find your niche. Specializing can open up diverse career opportunities.
→ **Continuous Learning:** The tech field evolves rapidly. Stay updated with the latest trends, tools, and technologies by following industry news, reading research papers, and taking advanced courses.